HARDCORE

F**K DEATH

WORKBOOK

An Honest Journal for Getting Through Grief Without the Condolences, Sympathy, and Other BS

STEVE CASE

This publication is designed to provide accurate and authoritative information in regard
to the subject matter covered. It is sold with the understanding that the publisher is
not engaged in rendering legal, accounting, or other professional service. If legal advice
or other expert assistance is required, the services of a competent professional person
should be sought. —*From a Declaration of Principles Jointly Adopted by a Committee
of the American Bar Association and a Committee of Publishers and Associations*

This book is not intended as a substitute for medical advice from a qualified
physician. The intent of this book is to provide accurate general information in
regard to the subject matter covered. If medical advice or other expert help is
needed, the services of an appropriate medical professional should be sought.

All biblical verses are used as reflected in the New International
Version (NIV) of the Christian Bible unless otherwise noted.

Published by Sourcebooks
P.O. Box 4410, Naperville, Illinois 60567–4410
(630) 961-3900
sourcebooks.com

Printed and bound in the United States of America.
AMZ

CONTENTS

INTRODUCTION

To begin, let's just say what we're all thinking right now:

FUCK THIS.

If you are reading this, it means one of the worst things in your life has just happened. Someone close to you has died.

And this sucks. This sucks a lot.

We're going to be honest. Blunt. Okay, we are going to swear—A LOT. It helps. Trust us, it helps. And we're going to give you some exercises to actually help you work through some of the things going through your head and your heart.

Will this book give you answers? Some, but probably not the kind you're looking for.

Will this book make you feel better? Some, but probably not the way you want.

But seriously, do you WANT to feel better right now?

OR

Do you want to punch somebody in the face until they feel as badly as you do?

This book isn't here to "make you better." It's here to understand. It's here to walk by your side and lead you through some things you might be feeling. It's here to be a shoulder to lean on without the cloying sympathy and anger-inducing condolences. It's simply here for you.

We get it: you don't want to go through this. You don't want to be using this workbook—a companion to *F**k Death*. But here we are. Hopefully, this workbook will be the shoulder you need while you sit with your grief. We're not here to solve all your problems or pretend this really bad shit didn't happen.

We are going to be blunt and profane. We are also going to be honest.

And we're going to ask you to try really hard to answer these questions. And do your best with these exercises.

Are you ready to start?

Tough shit. Here we go.

A Brief Reminder on the Five Stages of Grief and What They Actually Mean

DENIAL: No Fucking Way.

ANGER: Fuck. This.

BARGAINING: Let's Make a Fucking Deal.

DEPRESSION: Leave Me the Fuck Alone.

ACCEPTANCE: Embrace the Suckage.

DENIAL

(NO FUCKING WAY)

Somebody probably handed you this book. Hopefully, you didn't hit them with it or throw it across the room. Maybe you did. It's okay. They'll forgive you. Something horrible has happened or is about to happen, and you have no idea how to deal with it. You know that feeling when you lean back in your chair and then lean a little too far? That moment before you lose your balance and then get it back. That moment? That's your life right now. We're going to use the book to help you get your balance back.

Which one is more true? Check one.

❏	Your reflection in a mirror	❏	Your picture from a camera
❏	The book	❏	The movie
❏	The Bible	❏	Wikipedia
❏	Shipping estimates on Amazon	❏	Weight loss infomercials
❏	Serving suggestions on a pint of ice cream	❏	The nutrition information on a box of donuts
❏	Religion	❏	Ads on TV during an election year
❏	What people say	❏	What people do
❏	Someone you know has died	❏	That someone is in the next room playing a bad joke

NOTE: If you hesitated at all on that last one, even a little, even for a moment, we have some work to do.

In the space below, draw yourself, and highlight where you feel your grief physically. (It doesn't matter if you're a shitty artist. Just put something on the page.) Is it an ache in your chest, a sinking in your stomach, a twisting in your head?

What do you make of these signals? What are they telling you about your current mental and emotional state?

Do you think grief comes to us, or do we need to go find it?

What does denial mean to you? Have you denied your grief? How?

How is running from your pain or living in denial like running from your shadow?

Let's think about the present moment.

How do your hands feel?

Look at your surroundings. How do they smell? How many times have you been here? What else do you notice about it?

How does your body feel in this moment?

What has your brain been up to? What have your emotions physically felt like? What do they look like?

What is something you see right now that sticks out to you?

What do you hear?

What is it like to be totally present in this moment?

Now, let's take it a step further.

Think/talk about the person you lost. Think about their physicality. How did they smell? What was it like to hug them? Hold their hand? Be screamed at by them?

What was it like when you first met?

When you first laughed with them?

Say something about their hair.

How did they chew?

What was that one quirky thing they always seemed to do?

How did they brush their teeth?

Talk about their favorite pair of pants or other article of clothing.

How did they cut their meat or eat at a restaurant?

Where did they love to vacation?

What did they love above all else?

What are you going to miss?

Being present in the moment is one step closer to banishing your denial. It helps you unpack your current emotional landscape and truly confront your loss for the first time.

Notice the emptiness left by the person you lost. Draw an empty jar or box and then fill it with things you remember about that person. Nothing is too small—their perfume, the color of their favorite shirt, anything.

If only wonderful and amazing things happen to you, you will never learn to be brave.

What else would you never learn if you didn't face hard times?

DENIAL JOURNAL

ANGER

(FUCK. THIS.)

It's okay to be angry. Your friends will understand—your REAL friends that is. Others may not. It's easy to damage relationships in this stage. But you'll get through it and mend those fences later on. Right now, you are allowed to be angry...but you can't live here. You may be tempted to fill some of the empty space with dangerous behavior. Be mindful that this is temporary. This is a stage of grief; you must actively work to get through, but you are ALLOWED to be angry.

Rate the statements below on a scale from 1 to 10 with 1 being "Minor annoyance" to 10 being "If I had a rocket launcher, I'd make somebody pay."

.... People who enter in through the OUT door and try to exit through the IN door.

.... People who look at the McDonald's menu like it's the first time they've seen it.

.... People who make major life decisions based on a meme their uncle sent.

.... Cliffhangers.

.... Spoilers.

.... Not knowing the answers.

.... The next person who tells you it's all part of God's plan.

.... Relatives who talk like they've been there since the beginning of the problem.

.... The asshole who picked out that tie/dress/suit/coffin for the person who died.

.... The person who died for making you feel this way.

.... You, for letting this happen.

Personify grief. Is it a troll with bad breath and toe fungus? Is it a giant who's trying to slap you down? Describe grief as a character, and draw or write about it here.

Rip out a blank sheet from the back of this book. Draw a picture of a monster by the name of Anger. Be as detailed as you can. Feet, face, hair, expression, skin: What does anger look like? How does it compare to your Grief character?

If you don't want to draw, write the word "ANGER" in the middle of the page. You can choose any term(s) you want (RAGE, IRRITATION, FUCKING LIVID) that means the same thing.

When you're done drawing or writing, fold the page in half. Now fold the sheet in half again. Keep folding the page until you can't fold it anymore. If you have to, pound it on the table to make the fold-crease stay in place.

Set the paper aside.

What are some of the triggers of your anger right now?

What is one instance that really pissed you off?

Anger is like an iceberg. You think you're dealing with the sharp point, but beneath it is a whole host of other emotions that are fueling your anger. Can you name some of the emotions that are hiding beneath your anger right now?

How do you tend to deal with rage? Do you have any coping mechanisms you turn to?

How has anger affected your relationships lately? How has it affected your relationship with yourself?

Have you been on the other side of anyone's anger lately? What has that felt like?

Who are you most angry with right now? Why?

If you could cuss out one person right now, what would you say? Go ahead—write it all down on the fucking page.

Anger is easy. To be angry at the right time, at the right person, in the right amount—that takes some skill. Not everyone can pull that off.

Holding on to anger is like grabbing a hot rock to throw at someone else. Who gets burned?

Anger comes from fear. Ever see anyone on television screaming about the "they" or the "them" or the "those people"? Why are they angry?

Which is easier to handle, anger or grief?

Which would you rather deal with right now?

☐ Anger	☐ Grief
☐ Anger	☐ Tears
☐ Anger	☐ Guilt

.

Find something and throw it against the wall. Seriously, go find something that you can throw in a safe space. It can be a Slurpee against a dumpster. A book against a wall. THIS book against a wall.

Don't just turn the page. Stop reading and complete this task. Write down what you did in the space below with as much detail as possible.

What sound did it make?

Where did you do it?

Did you have a mess to clean when you were done?

Force yourself to move very slowly. Make your hands unfold that piece of paper you folded up so tightly. Slowly. When the paper is unfolded, carefully tear out the word/ picture and slip it into the pages as a bookmark for this chapter. You might want to come back to it later.

Carrying anger around is like carrying a large box or laundry basket under one arm everywhere you go: eventually, it starts to get in the way.

Let go of the box. How does that feel?

ANGER JOURNAL

BARGAINING

(Let's Make a Fucking Deal)

There is a piece of good news here. Just a little bit of good fucking news that you could probably use right now, right? It may not seem like it, but if you are in this stage, if you are playing the "if only" game, if you are making promises and deals with your higher power, that means you have acknowledged that the someone you love is not coming back. Yes, that sucks, but it's progress. It's a forward movement. Sometimes a micro-movement is still a movement. Understand this, it's essential: you are not going to get what you want out of this. The person you lost is not coming back. You are not going to feel better (yet). You are not going to get answers (not the ones you want, anyway). You are playing a high-stakes game of poker, and someone has dealt you cards from Candyland. Princess Lolly is a bitch, and she's not going to make it easy. You are not going to sweep the table.

But you are going to get through this phase.

Would you rather (check one):

❏ Eat a bag of M&Ms all by yourself	❏	Share the yellow ones.
❏ Binge-watch your favorite show	❏	Wait a week between episodes to savor the anticipation
❏ Put "tire-damage" spikes in the grocery store parking lot for the idiots who don't understand ENTER-EXIT signs	❏	Shop at the grocery store all by yourself without screaming children and inconsiderate shoppers
❏ Start a frustrating errand	❏	Finish a frustrating errand
❏ Win at poker	❏	Lose on purpose to a child at Candyland
❏ Understand why the person you loved died	❏	Have proof they have moved on to something better
❏ Have one more conversation with the person you loved	❏	Know they died feeling loved and whole

DO

The sun is going to set tonight. If you are reading this at night, it's going to come up in the morning. Do you think there is one damn thing you can do to change that? You can want your loved one to be "not dead" as hard as you want. You can squeeze your eyes closed and wish with all your might. Guess what? All you did was give yourself a headache.

In the middle of the space below, draw a circle, big enough to write in but leave room on the outside as well. In the circle, write down ten things you are in complete control of. Outside of the circle, write down ten things you have no control of whatsoever. Take a deep breath and think about the differences between those lists.

Describe how the bargaining phase has affected your life.

What does bargaining look like to you?

Who/what are you speaking to during this phase? Who/what are you bartering with?

What other emotions are you feeling during this phase?

List three ways you can work to stop the bargaining mind-loop? What are those coping skills?

Grief is a fuck-face, asshat bastard. Grief is that idiot push-ing a shopping cart down the middle of the aisle at the supermarket. Just when you try to flip over to another sec-tion to get away from them, they show up again. Grief is the tailgater with his brights on in your mirror, blinking like you are going to get out of his way on a single lane highway. You're not going to get away from grief.

When negotiating a deal, some advisers will tell you to lead with your highest ask—something outlandish even—so that when the bargaining is over, you've reached a middle ground, getting exactly what you wanted in the first place.

Can you think of five things that are completely non-negotiable for you, no matter how crazy they might seem to someone else?

Bargaining with God or the universe or any higher power is fucking pointless. They already have everything. Thinking the universe owes you something is a waste of time. It was here first.

Have you offered your higher power anything during this whole process? What was it? Write it down in the space below.

You are not yourself during this process. You're going to think of yourself in a lot of unusual ways, but they are not you. You are not stupid. You are not an asshole. You are not at fault. You are not yourself. You are just fucking desperate for some relief.

More than likely you've thought some truly horrible things. You may even have said some of them out loud. This is typical. Don't beat yourself up about it, and don't keep a record of them. You are not yourself. Who would you like to be right now?

Why do you think bargaining is so common that it's included in the stages of grief? Why does everyone do it?

Have you come up with any new ideas during this process? In all your thoughts about what you would do or wouldn't do if the universe would just change, if time could roll back, if God would just grant you this wish? What have you realized? (You can come back to this later if you want.)

Right now, your heart is playing a scene over and over, hoping for a different outcome.

Is there a scene from a movie you've seen so many times that you know it by heart? Go watch that scene now, play it several times, and see if you can spot or hear something you've never noticed before.

Offer forgiveness—to yourself, those around you, and the one who is gone. You can't bargain your way out of this, and the outcome won't change.

Is there an outcome you can change right now? What?

BARGAINING JOURNAL

DEPRESSION

(Leave Me the Fuck Alone)

Depression is a hole, and the hole is deep. We burrow down, not because we are trying to find something, but because everything above us hurts. Happy people, music, sometimes even light just hurts. Down here in the hole, nothing can get to us. Silent. Peaceful. Dark. You can stay down here in the hole you have dug for as long as you want, as long as you need, but you can't *stay* down forever. You need to climb out at some point to finally feel free.

True or false:

This sucks.	❏ True	❏ False
This sucks a lot.	❏ True	❏ False
This sucks pretty much more than anything has ever sucked before.	❏ True	❏ False
This sucks more than that one time _____.	❏ True	❏ False
Life is hard, then you die.	❏ True	❏ False
It's going to feel this shitty forever.	❏ True	❏ False

LISTEN

A good friend will have the ability to just sit with you and shut the hell up. Too often we feel the need to fill the silence. It takes real friendship to just "be" there. In silence and confusion, to just sit and stay is a gift.

Do you have a friend who can just shut up and sit with you? Who is it?

Have you ever been that kind of friend? When?

Take out your phone or your calendar and set an appointment for six months from this moment right now. Make a reminder to call the friend who helped you or write them a thank-you note.

How is time working for you today? Does it seem like the days drag? Does it seem like the days drag while you are in them, but if you look back, you think "Where did the time go?" Pay attention to time for the next few minutes. Look at your watch or set a timer for sixty seconds and count your breaths. Write about that experience here.

Draw a scale. Not bathroom scale but the "Lady Justice" statue kind with the fulcrum and the plates on either side.

On one side of the scale, write the word "death."

On the other side, write as many words as you want to counter the weight of death. Keep adding words until you feel you have a balance.

When is the hardest time of day for you right now? Why?

What does your depression feel like?

What does your support system look like right now? Who is that friend who will just sit and shut the hell up with you?

When you're alone with your thoughts, how does it feel?

Describe your grief. Write down in as much detail as possible what your grief has looked like.

How do you think you're coping?

What is something you wish your friends or family would say or do right now?

When my mother died, I was there beside her. My father had one hand and I had the other, and she quietly drifted away on us. I didn't cry. I made it through the funeral and the following week of sorting her stuff with barely a tear. I was working for a church at the time, and when I returned to my office, a child in the Sunday school class had made me a homemade sympathy card. It was a picture of a butterfly, and it said, "I'm sorry your mommy died." I stood in the hallway and blubbered like a baby.

What has been your trigger? What set you off when you thought you had it under control?

What is your outlet for your emotions? Painting? Singing? Cooking? If it's something you can practice here, fill the rest of this page with it.

If not, go do your own thing for a while, then come back and write about how it felt.

Have you ever listened to sad music because you were sad? Or does letting sunlight in a dark place make it better?

What is the most "healing" song for you right now? One that plays in your mind when you feel down. The one that mysteriously plays when you most need to hear it. Write down some of the words in the space below. Is there one specific line that you find comforting? Write that one line down as many times as you have space for.

Indulge completely in the sad, but then tell it to fuck off so you can get out of bed.

You can do it. Get out of bed.

DEPRESSION JOURNAL

ACCEPTANCE

(Embrace the Suckage)

YOU ARE HERE. You exist. You are able to step outside and breathe air into your lungs and look at the sky. You can pick out the colors in the sunset and sunrise. You can count the stars until you get tired of counting. That's a good thing—you've reached the acceptance phase. From here, you can do almost anything. The world is open to you. This is all new. It doesn't mean everything is all hunky-dory. It doesn't mean you are happy. It doesn't mean you won't cry anymore. You've reached this chapter; you understand why you are here. Hard truth: It's never going to be like it was before. Easier truth: You get to keep going.

Which is more important?

❏	Dreams	❏	Facts
❏	Stories	❏	History
❏	Past	❏	Future
❏	Hope	❏	Experience
❏	Laughter	❏	Tears
❏	Love	❏	Death

Look at how you answered the above. What do you think your answers say about your current mindset? Write about the importance of the answers you *didn't* pick.

Grab a pen or pencil and draw a house after a hurricane blows through.

Who would you enlist to help you rebuild that shit?

If you think of yourself as a house, what's your roof? What's keeping you protected from the storm?

You are standing on the porch of your rebuilt house. Different walls, different roof, different floor. This is a NEW place. This is not a do-over. You don't get one of those. This is a start-over. What makes it Home?

What do you hope to experience in the future? What is something you're looking forward to?

Have your goals changed during your grief? What is your goal for this year? For the next five years?

What are some of the differences you know you'll face without that person in your life?

What do you appreciate now more than you did before? Why?

What does hope mean to you?

When you think about that person who has died, what is your favorite memory? How does that memory make you feel?

What do you think moving on looks like? Chart your own path to moving forward.

Acceptance looks normal to the outside world. No one can tell that your house used to be fucked up. However, the fact is, it took a long time to get here. And things aren't the same, but they are going to be okay.

Acceptance changes the vibration you are putting out into the world. We're no longer talking about "things as they were." Now it's "things as they are."

You've got memories of the person you lost, lots and lots of them...perhaps a lifetime of them. Now you have to make new ones. You're going to have all kinds of memories that they will not be a part of. What does that feel like?

How long has it been since that person has died? Write the answer as exactly as you can.

Have you ever reached the point where you turned to an empty space to talk to them? Or reached to text or call? Or driven your car by their house and attempted to stop in? What did that feel like?

You might think, "You can't make me accept this. It's never going to be okay."

Those are actually two different things. Write down why they feel the same.

Now, write down some ways they are different.

What have you discovered about yourself?

Have you learned anything new about the person who died since they died?

Have you learned anything new about your family and friends?

It's possible to transform pain into remembrance. You can share the memories you still have. Other people can experience the person you're missing. When grief starts to become painful, it's time to start sharing the memories.

What are you remembering more than anything else?

Reflect on these facts:

With acceptance, what you have becomes enough.

Chaos becomes organization.

Ignorance becomes clarity.

A meal becomes a gathering.

A house becomes a home.

A stranger becomes a friend.

Loss becomes gratitude.

Write down five things you are grateful for right now.

Fear and anger cause tunnel vision. You can't see the world around you offering solutions. Acceptance lets you see the situation for what it is. Acceptance isn't the end of the problem. Acceptance lets you see the options forward.

Think about where you were when you started. Go back and look at those pages if you want to. Is "tunnel vision" accurate? What do you notice about the space around you now?

Acceptance makes room for patience and faith. Look realistically at the world around you. Choose a direction and have faith in yourself. What is your next destination? (You can be literal or metaphorical.) Where are you going from here? Why is it important?

Very carefully tear out another page. Write down where and how you want to move forward. Fold a paper airplane. Something simple or complicated, your choice. Fold it and then throw it from wherever you are sitting. Nice work. You're getting somewhere.

This is only the beginning. Buckle the fuck up. You're going places.

What does this phrase mean to you? How does it make you feel?

ACCEPTANCE JOURNAL

THINGS WE TOTALLY DON'T UNDERSTAND

There is no such thing as "all better" when it comes to grief. There is "better than it was," there is "better than yesterday," but there is not "all better." Grief is never really finished, but the pain eases and help arrives. Imagine yourself floating alone in the ocean. How long can you tread water? Then you find a flotation device and grab on. Is it going to erase the horror of the shipwreck that put you in the water in the first place? No, but it will help, and you know you'll survive. With help, you will survive.

What does that help look like? Is there a higher power

that you can turn to? This is when we get into the things we don't totally understand. The faith stuff. How does that play into your grief? How has it pulled you out of it? That's what we're going to explore.

Grief knocks you around so hard, it can be impossible to know your ass from your elbow, let alone what "normal" feels like. Rank these tasks on a scale from 1 to 10, with 1 being "I can do that right now" and 10 being "You're out of your mind if you think I'm getting that done."

_____ Get a haircut.

_____ Wash the dishes.

_____ Go for a walk.

_____ Tap dance on the stairs.

_____ Talk to a stranger.

_____ Pray.

_____ Visit your favorite place with that person.

_____ Meditate.

_____ Make a meal.

_____ Get groceries.

_____ Sing their favorite song.

_____ Paint a picture.

_____ Ride a mechanical bull.

_____ Call a friend to chat.

Now, pick a 1, and go do it. Let yourself feel normal while you do your activity.

In the space below, write the name of the person who died. Now draw a box around it. Use a little creativity and make the box a treasure chest. Color the box in. Draw a lock.

This is your treasure chest. Anytime you want, you can come open it. It'll have the grief you've felt for this person, but you need to stop carrying it around. Return any time you want, but don't take it with you.

What is the key that will let you back in? Why would you want to visit again?

Embrace the suckage. Grief really fucking sucks. Let it suck.

What was the last time you experienced an emotion fully with 100 percent immersion? It doesn't have to be pain or sadness; it can be joy or fear or determination. What was that experience like?

Now think about what comes next. What do you want your journey forward to look like?

Would you rather test the pool by dipping in your big toe or doing a cannonball off the high dive?

What happens when you put up walls around you? You smile when you want to cry. You pretend to be nice to people who are assholes. How does it make you feel? What does it accomplish?

Grief and acceptance are part of the natural cycle of things. Breaking and healing. One follows the other.

Imagine you're a vase. Someone dropped you. How have you put yourself back together? What glue are you using?

What does faith mean to you? How has faith played a part in your grief?

Do you have a higher power? What does it look like? How have you turned to it?

Is it possible to fully appreciate a person while they are still here? What did you love most about the person you lost while they were alive? Is that still the top of your list?

What have you learned to appreciate about your friends and family during this process?

Do you think our loved ones live on in us? How the fuck does that work?

Who has helped you the most during your grief? How would you like to thank them today?

What has your higher power taught you during this process?

Write yourself a note here talking about your grief, your loved one, and what you've learned. At some point, you will come back to this page. It could be years from now. It could be tomorrow. You might pass the book on to someone else. You could write them a note as well. But write something here and leave it all out on the page.

Grief makes room. Let love fill it.

How can you let love fill the room today?

F**K DEATH
Journal

Made in the USA
Las Vegas, NV
11 October 2021